This planner belongs to :

_____

Twenty-three

January

S	M	T	W	T	F	S
1	2	3	4	5	6	7
8	9	10	11	12	13	14
15	16	17	18	19	20	21
22	23	24	25	26	27	28
29	30	31				

February

S	M	T	W	T	F	S
			1	2	3	4
5	6	7	8	9	10	11
12	13	14	15	16	17	18
19	20	21	22	23	24	25
26	27	28				

March

S	M	T	W	T	F	S
			1	2	3	4
5	6	7	8	9	10	11
12	13	14	15	16	17	18
19	20	21	22	23	24	25
26	27	28	29	30	31	

April

S	M	T	W	T	F	S
						1
2	3	4	5	6	7	8
9	10	11	12	13	14	15
16	17	18	19	20	21	22
23	24	25	26	27	28	29
30						

May

S	M	T	W	T	F	S
	1	2	3	4	5	6
7	8	9	10	11	12	13
14	15	16	17	18	19	20
21	22	23	24	25	26	27
28	29	30	31			

June

S	M	T	W	T	F	S
				1	2	3
4	5	6	7	8	9	10
11	12	13	14	15	16	17
18	19	20	21	22	23	24
25	26	27	28	29	30	

July

S	M	T	W	T	F	S
						1
2	3	4	5	6	7	8
9	10	11	12	13	14	15
16	17	18	19	20	21	22
23	24	25	26	27	28	29
30	31					

August

S	M	T	W	T	F	S
		1	2	3	4	5
6	7	8	9	10	11	12
13	14	15	16	17	18	19
20	21	22	23	24	25	26
27	28	29	30	31		

September

S	M	T	W	T	F	S
					1	2
3	4	5	6	7	8	9
10	11	12	13	14	15	16
17	18	19	20	21	22	23
24	25	26	27	28	29	30

October

S	M	T	W	T	F	S
1	2	3	4	5	6	7
8	9	10	11	12	13	14
15	16	17	18	19	20	21
22	23	24	25	26	27	28
29	30	31				

November

S	M	T	W	T	F	S
			1	2	3	4
5	6	7	8	9	10	11
12	13	14	15	16	17	18
19	20	21	22	23	24	25
26	27	28	29	30		

December

S	M	T	W	T	F	S
					1	2
3	4	5	6	7	8	9
10	11	12	13	14	15	16
17	18	19	20	21	22	23
24	25	26	27	28	29	30
31						

Year in Pixels

	J	F	M	A	M	J	J	A	S	O	N	D
1.												
2.												
3.												
4.												
5.												
6.												
7.												
8.												
9.												
10.												
11.												
12.												
13.												
14.												
15.												
16.												
17.												
18.												
19.												
20.												
21.												
22.												
23.												
24.												
25.												
26.												
27.												
28.												
29.												
30.												
31.												

Color Codes

Notes

January

MONDAY	TUESDAY	WEDNESDAY	THURSDAY
2	3	4	5
9	10	11	12
16	17	18	19
23	24	25	26

January

FRIDAY	SATURDAY	SUNDAY	NOTES
		1	○
			○
			○
			○
			○
6	7	8	○
			○
			○
			○
13	14	15	○
			○
			○
			○
			○
20	21	22	○
			○
			○
			○
			○
27	28	29	30
			31

February

MONDAY	TUESDAY	WEDNESDAY	THURSDAY
		1	2
6	7	8	9
13	14	15	16
20	21	22	23
27	28		

February

FRIDAY	SATURDAY	SUNDAY	NOTES
3	4	5	○
			○
			○
			○
			○
10	11	12	○
			○
			○
			○
			○
17	18	19	○
			○
			○
			○
			○
24	25	26	○
			○
			○
			○
			○
			NOTES

March 2023

MONDAY	TUESDAY	WEDNESDAY	THURSDAY
		1	2
6	7	8	9
13	14	15	16
20	21	22	23
27	28	29	30

March

2023

FRIDAY	SATURDAY	SUNDAY	NOTES
3	4	5	○
			○
			○
			○
			○
10	11	12	○
			○
			○
			○
			○
17	18	19	○
			○
			○
			○
24	25	26	○
			○
			○
			○
			○
31			NOTES

April 2023

MONDAY	TUESDAY	WEDNESDAY	THURSDAY
3	4	5	6
10	11	12	13
17	18	19	20
24	25	26	27

April

FRIDAY	SATURDAY	SUNDAY	NOTES
	1	2	○
			○
			○
			○
			○
7	8	9	○
			○
			○
			○
14	15	16	○
			○
			○
			○
			○
21	22	23	○
			○
			○
			○
			○
28	29	30	NOTES

May

2023

MONDAY	TUESDAY	WEDNESDAY	THURSDAY
1	2	3	4
8	9	10	11
15	16	17	18
22	23	24	25
29	30	31	

May

FRIDAY	SATURDAY	SUNDAY	NOTES
5	6	7	○
			○
			○
			○
			○
12	13	14	○
			○
			○
			○
			○
19	20	21	○
			○
			○
			○
			○
26	27	28	○
			○
			○
			○
			○
			NOTES

June 2023

MONDAY	TUESDAY	WEDNESDAY	THURSDAY
			1
5	6	7	8
12	13	14	15
19	20	21	22
26	27	28	29

June

2023

FRIDAY	SATURDAY	SUNDAY	NOTES
2	3	4	○
			○
			○
			○
			○
9	10	11	○
			○
			○
			○
			○
16	17	18	○
			○
			○
			○
			○
23	24	25	○
			○
			○
			○
			○
30			NOTES

July

2023

MONDAY	TUESDAY	WEDNESDAY	THURSDAY
3	4	5	6
10	11	12	13
17	18	19	20
24	25	26	27

July

FRIDAY	SATURDAY	SUNDAY	NOTES
	1	2	○
			○
			○
			○
			○
7	8	9	○
			○
			○
			○
14	15	16	○
			○
			○
			○
			○
21	22	23	○
			○
			○
			○
			○
28	29	30	31

August

2023

MONDAY	TUESDAY	WEDNESDAY	THURSDAY
	1	2	3
7	8	9	10
14	15	16	17
21	22	23	24
28	29	30	31

August

FRIDAY	SATURDAY	SUNDAY	NOTES
4	5	6	○
			○
			○
			○
			○
11	12	13	○
			○
			○
			○
			○
18	19	20	○
			○
			○
			○
			○
25	26	27	NOTES

September

MONDAY	TUESDAY	WEDNESDAY	THURSDAY
4	5	6	7
11	12	13	14
18	19	20	21
25	26	27	28

September

FRIDAY	SATURDAY	SUNDAY	NOTES
1	2	3	○
			○
			○
			○
			○
8	9	10	○
			○
			○
			○
15	16	17	○
			○
			○
			○
			○
22	23	24	○
			○
			○
			○
			○
29	30		NOTES

October

MONDAY	TUESDAY	WEDNESDAY	THURSDAY
2	3	4	5
9	10	11	12
16	17	18	19
23	24	25	26

October  2023

FRIDAY	SATURDAY	SUNDAY	NOTES
		1	○
			○
			○
			○
6	7	8	○
			○
			○
			○
13	14	15	○
			○
			○
			○
			○
20	21	22	○
			○
			○
			○
			○
27	28	29	30 / 31

November

MONDAY	TUESDAY	WEDNESDAY	THURSDAY
		1	2
6	7	8	9
13	14	15	16
20	21	22	23
27	28	29	30

November

FRIDAY	SATURDAY	SUNDAY	NOTES
3	4	5	○
			○
			○
			○
			○
10	11	12	○
			○
			○
			○
			○
17	18	19	○
			○
			○
			○
			○
24	25	26	○
			○
			○
			○
			○
			NOTES

December

MONDAY	TUESDAY	WEDNESDAY	THURSDAY
4	5	6	7
11	12	13	14
18	19	20	21
25	26	27	28

December

FRIDAY	SATURDAY	SUNDAY	NOTES
1	2	3	○
			○
			○
			○
			○
8	9	10	○
			○
			○
			○
			○
15	16	17	○
			○
			○
			○
			○
22	23	24	○
			○
			○
			○
			○
29	30	31	NOTES

December
2022

01 THURSDAY
- ○
- ○
- ○
- ○
- ○
- ○
- ○
- ○

02 FRIDAY
- ○
- ○
- ○
- ○
- ○
- ○
- ○
- ○

03 SATURDAY
- ○
- ○
- ○
- ○
- ○
- ○
- ○
- ○

04 SUNDAY
- ○
- ○
- ○
- ○
- ○

December
2022

05 MONDAY

06 TUESDAY

07 WEDNESDAY

08 THURSDAY

December
2022

09 FRIDAY

○
○
○
○
○
○
○
○

10 SATURDAY

○
○
○
○
○
○
○
○

11 SUNDAY

○
○
○
○
○
○
○
○

12 MONDAY

○
○
○
○
○

December
2022

13 TUESDAY

14 WEDNESDAY

15 THURSDAY

16 FRIDAY

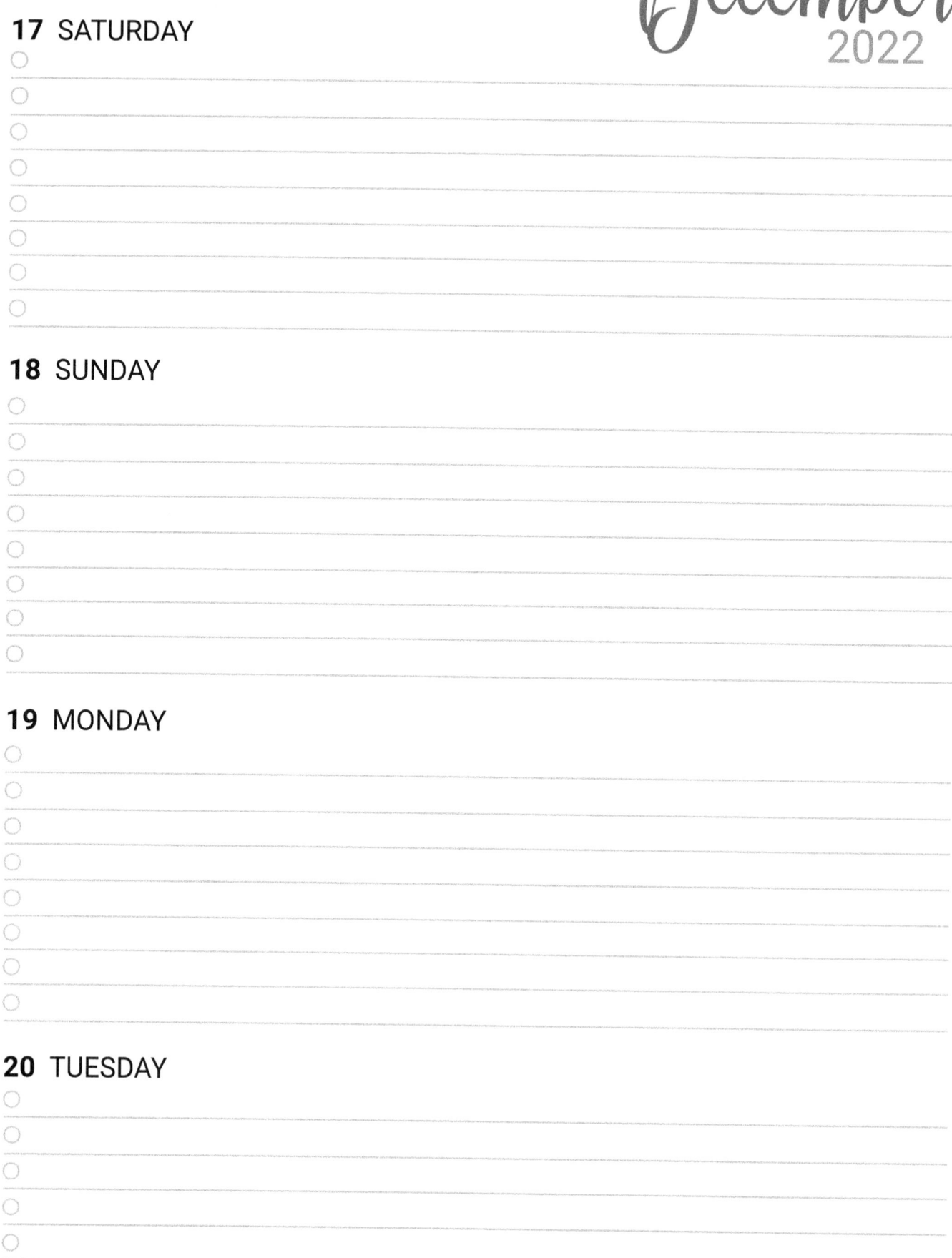

December
2022

17 SATURDAY

18 SUNDAY

19 MONDAY

20 TUESDAY

December
2022

21 WEDNESDAY

22 THURSDAY

23 FRIDAY

24 SATURDAY

December
2022

25 SUNDAY

○
○
○
○
○
○
○
○

26 MONDAY

○
○
○
○
○
○
○
○

27 TUESDAY

○
○
○
○
○
○
○
○

28 WEDNESDAY

○
○
○
○
○

December
2022

29 THURSDAY

30 FRIDAY

31 SATURDAY

NOTES

January
2023

01 SUNDAY

02 MONDAY

03 TUESDAY

04 WEDNESDAY

05 THURSDAY

06 FRIDAY

07 SATURDAY

08 SUNDAY

09 MONDAY

○
○
○
○
○
○
○
○

10 TUESDAY

○
○
○
○
○
○
○
○

11 WEDNESDAY

○
○
○
○
○
○
○
○

12 THURSDAY

○
○
○
○
○

13 FRIDAY

14 SATURDAY

15 SUNDAY

16 MONDAY

17 TUESDAY

18 WEDNESDAY

19 THURSDAY

20 FRIDAY

21 SATURDAY

22 SUNDAY

23 MONDAY

24 TUESDAY

25 WEDNESDAY

26 THURSDAY

27 FRIDAY

28 SATURDAY

29 SUNDAY

30 MONDAY

31 TUESDAY

NOTES

01 WEDNESDAY

- ○
- ○
- ○
- ○
- ○
- ○
- ○
- ○

02 THURSDAY

- ○
- ○
- ○
- ○
- ○
- ○
- ○
- ○

03 FRIDAY

- ○
- ○
- ○
- ○
- ○
- ○
- ○
- ○

04 SATURDAY

- ○
- ○
- ○
- ○

February 2023

05 SUNDAY

06 MONDAY

07 TUESDAY

08 WEDNESDAY

February
2023

09 THURSDAY

○
○
○
○
○
○
○
○

10 FRIDAY

○
○
○
○
○
○
○
○

11 SATURDAY

○
○
○
○
○
○
○
○

12 SUNDAY

○
○
○
○
○

February 2023

13 MONDAY

14 TUESDAY

15 WEDNESDAY

16 THURSDAY

17 FRIDAY

18 SATURDAY

19 SUNDAY

20 MONDAY

February
2023

21 TUESDAY

22 WEDNESDAY

23 THURSDAY

24 FRIDAY

25 SATURDAY

26 SUNDAY

27 MONDAY

28 TUESDAY

March
2023

01 WEDNESDAY

02 THURSDAY

03 FRIDAY

04 SATURDAY

March 2023

05 SUNDAY

- ○ _____
- ○ _____
- ○ _____
- ○ _____
- ○ _____
- ○ _____
- ○ _____

06 MONDAY

- ○ _____
- ○ _____
- ○ _____
- ○ _____
- ○ _____
- ○ _____
- ○ _____
- ○ _____

07 TUESDAY

- ○ _____
- ○ _____
- ○ _____
- ○ _____
- ○ _____
- ○ _____
- ○ _____
- ○ _____

08 WEDNESDAY

- ○ _____
- ○ _____
- ○ _____
- ○ _____
- ○ _____

09 THURSDAY

10 FRIDAY

11 SATURDAY

12 SUNDAY

13 MONDAY

○
○
○
○
○
○
○
○

14 TUESDAY

○
○
○
○
○
○
○
○

15 WEDNESDAY

○
○
○
○
○
○
○
○

16 THURSDAY

○
○
○
○
○

17 FRIDAY

18 SATURDAY

19 SUNDAY

20 MONDAY

March
2023

21 TUESDAY

22 WEDNESDAY

23 THURSDAY

24 FRIDAY

25 SATURDAY

26 SUNDAY

27 MONDAY

28 TUESDAY

29 WEDNESDAY

○
○
○
○
○
○
○
○

30 THURSDAY

○
○
○
○
○
○
○
○

31 FRIDAY

○
○
○
○
○
○
○
○

NOTES

01 SATURDAY

02 SUNDAY

03 MONDAY

04 TUESDAY

April
2023

05 WEDNESDAY

06 THURSDAY

07 FRIDAY

08 SATURDAY

April
2023

09 SUNDAY

10 MONDAY

11 TUESDAY

12 WEDNESDAY

13 THURSDAY

14 FRIDAY

15 SATURDAY

16 SUNDAY

April
2023

17 MONDAY

○
○
○
○
○
○
○

18 TUESDAY

○
○
○
○
○
○
○
○

19 WEDNESDAY

○
○
○
○
○
○
○

20 THURSDAY

○
○
○
○
○

April
2023

21 FRIDAY

○
○
○
○
○
○
○
○

22 SATURDAY

○
○
○
○
○
○
○
○

23 SUNDAY

○
○
○
○
○
○
○
○

24 MONDAY

○
○
○
○
○

25 TUESDAY

26 WEDNESDAY

27 THURSDAY

28 FRIDAY

April
2023

29 SATURDAY
○
○
○
○
○
○
○
○

30 SUNDAY
○
○
○
○
○
○
○
○

NOTES

May
2023

01 MONDAY

02 TUESDAY

03 WEDNESDAY

04 THURSDAY

May 2023

05 FRIDAY
○
○
○
○
○
○
○

06 SATURDAY
○
○
○
○
○
○
○
○

07 SUNDAY
○
○
○
○
○
○
○
○

08 MONDAY
○
○
○
○
○

May
2023

09 TUESDAY

10 WEDNESDAY

11 THURSDAY

12 FRIDAY

May
2023

13 SATURDAY

○
○
○
○
○
○
○
○

14 SUNDAY

○
○
○
○
○
○
○
○

15 MONDAY

○
○
○
○
○
○
○
○

16 TUESDAY

○
○
○
○
○

May
2023

17 WEDNESDAY

18 THURSDAY

19 FRIDAY

20 SATURDAY

May
2023

21 SUNDAY

22 MONDAY

23 TUESDAY

24 WEDNESDAY

25 THURSDAY

26 FRIDAY

27 SATURDAY

28 SUNDAY

May
2023

29 MONDAY

○ _____
○ _____
○ _____
○ _____
○ _____
○ _____
○ _____
○ _____

30 TUESDAY

○ _____
○ _____
○ _____
○ _____
○ _____
○ _____
○ _____
○ _____

31 WEDNESDAY

○ _____
○ _____
○ _____
○ _____
○ _____
○ _____
○ _____
○ _____

NOTES

_____
_____
_____
_____

June
2023

01 THURSDAY

02 FRIDAY

03 SATURDAY

04 SUNDAY

05 MONDAY

○

○

○

○

○

○

○

○

06 TUESDAY

○

○

○

○

○

○

○

○

07 WEDNESDAY

○

○

○

○

○

○

○

○

08 THURSDAY

○

○

○

○

○

09 FRIDAY

10 SATURDAY

11 SUNDAY

12 MONDAY

13 TUESDAY

14 WEDNESDAY

15 THURSDAY

16 FRIDAY

17 SATURDAY

18 SUNDAY

19 MONDAY

20 TUESDAY

21 WEDNESDAY

- ○
- ○
- ○
- ○
- ○
- ○
- ○
- ○

22 THURSDAY

- ○
- ○
- ○
- ○
- ○
- ○
- ○
- ○

23 FRIDAY

- ○
- ○
- ○
- ○
- ○
- ○
- ○
- ○

24 SATURDAY

- ○
- ○
- ○
- ○
- ○

June 2023

25 SUNDAY

26 MONDAY

27 TUESDAY

28 WEDNESDAY

29 THURSDAY
○
○
○
○
○
○
○
○

30 FRIDAY
○
○
○
○
○
○
○
○

NOTES

July
2023

01 SATURDAY

02 SUNDAY

03 MONDAY

04 TUESDAY

05 WEDNESDAY

○ _____
○ _____
○ _____
○ _____
○ _____
○ _____
○ _____

06 THURSDAY

○ _____
○ _____
○ _____
○ _____
○ _____
○ _____
○ _____

07 FRIDAY

○ _____
○ _____
○ _____
○ _____
○ _____
○ _____
○ _____

08 SATURDAY

○ _____
○ _____
○ _____
○ _____

July
2023

09 SUNDAY

10 MONDAY

11 TUESDAY

12 WEDNESDAY

13 THURSDAY

○
○
○
○
○
○
○
○

14 FRIDAY

○
○
○
○
○
○
○
○

15 SATURDAY

○
○
○
○
○
○
○
○

16 SUNDAY

○
○
○
○
○

17 MONDAY

18 TUESDAY

19 WEDNESDAY

20 THURSDAY

21 FRIDAY

○
○
○
○
○
○
○

22 SATURDAY

○
○
○
○
○
○
○
○

23 SUNDAY

○
○
○
○
○
○
○

24 MONDAY

○
○
○
○
○

25 TUESDAY

26 WEDNESDAY

27 THURSDAY

28 FRIDAY

July
2023

29 SATURDAY
- ○
- ○
- ○
- ○
- ○
- ○
- ○
- ○

30 SUNDAY
- ○
- ○
- ○
- ○
- ○
- ○
- ○
- ○

31 MONDAY
- ○
- ○
- ○
- ○
- ○
- ○
- ○
- ○

NOTES

August 2023

01 TUESDAY

○
○
○
○
○
○
○
○

02 WEDNESDAY

○
○
○
○
○
○
○
○

03 THURSDAY

○
○
○
○
○
○
○
○

04 FRIDAY

○
○
○
○
○

August
2023

05 SATURDAY

06 SUNDAY

07 MONDAY

08 TUESDAY

09 WEDNESDAY

10 THURSDAY

11 FRIDAY

12 SATURDAY

August
2023

13 SUNDAY

14 MONDAY

15 TUESDAY

16 WEDNESDAY

August
2023

17 THURSDAY

18 FRIDAY

19 SATURDAY

20 SUNDAY

21 MONDAY

22 TUESDAY

23 WEDNESDAY

24 THURSDAY

25 FRIDAY

26 SATURDAY

27 SUNDAY

28 MONDAY

August
2023

29 TUESDAY

○
○
○
○
○
○
○
○

30 WEDNESDAY

○
○
○
○
○
○
○
○

31 THURSDAY

○
○
○
○
○
○
○
○

NOTES

September
2023

01 FRIDAY

02 SATURDAY

03 SUNDAY

04 MONDAY

05 TUESDAY

○
○
○
○
○
○
○
○

06 WEDNESDAY

○
○
○
○
○
○
○
○

07 THURSDAY

○
○
○
○
○
○
○
○

08 FRIDAY

○
○
○
○
○

09 SATURDAY

10 SUNDAY

11 MONDAY

12 TUESDAY

13 WEDNESDAY

○
○
○
○
○
○
○

14 THURSDAY

○
○
○
○
○
○
○
○

15 FRIDAY

○
○
○
○
○
○
○

16 SATURDAY

○
○
○
○
○

17 SUNDAY

18 MONDAY

19 TUESDAY

20 WEDNESDAY

21 THURSDAY

○
○
○
○
○
○
○
○

22 FRIDAY

○
○
○
○
○
○
○
○

23 SATURDAY

○
○
○
○
○
○
○
○

24 SUNDAY

○
○
○
○
○

25 MONDAY

26 TUESDAY

27 WEDNESDAY

28 THURSDAY

29 FRIDAY

- ○
- ○
- ○
- ○
- ○
- ○
- ○
- ○

30 SATURDAY

- ○
- ○
- ○
- ○
- ○
- ○
- ○
- ○

NOTES

October
2023

01 SUNDAY

02 MONDAY

03 TUESDAY

04 WEDNESDAY

October
2023

05 THURSDAY

06 FRIDAY

07 SATURDAY

08 SUNDAY

October
2023

09 MONDAY

10 TUESDAY

11 WEDNESDAY

12 THURSDAY

October
2023

13 FRIDAY

14 SATURDAY

15 SUNDAY

16 MONDAY

October
2023

17 TUESDAY

18 WEDNESDAY

19 THURSDAY

20 FRIDAY

October
2023

21 SATURDAY

22 SUNDAY

23 MONDAY

24 TUESDAY

October
2023

25 WEDNESDAY

26 THURSDAY

27 FRIDAY

28 SATURDAY

October
2023

29 SUNDAY

30 MONDAY

31 TUESDAY

NOTES

November
2023

01 WEDNESDAY

02 THURSDAY

03 FRIDAY

04 SATURDAY

05 SUNDAY
- ○
- ○
- ○
- ○
- ○
- ○
- ○
- ○

06 MONDAY
- ○
- ○
- ○
- ○
- ○
- ○
- ○
- ○

07 TUESDAY
- ○
- ○
- ○
- ○
- ○
- ○
- ○
- ○

08 WEDNESDAY
- ○
- ○
- ○
- ○
- ○

November
2023

09 THURSDAY

10 FRIDAY

11 SATURDAY

12 SUNDAY

November
2023

13 MONDAY

14 TUESDAY

15 WEDNESDAY

16 THURSDAY

17 FRIDAY

18 SATURDAY

19 SUNDAY

20 MONDAY

November
2023

21 TUESDAY

○ _____
○ _____
○ _____
○ _____
○ _____
○ _____
○ _____
○ _____

22 WEDNESDAY

○ _____
○ _____
○ _____
○ _____
○ _____
○ _____
○ _____
○ _____

23 THURSDAY

○ _____
○ _____
○ _____
○ _____
○ _____
○ _____
○ _____
○ _____

24 FRIDAY

○ _____
○ _____
○ _____
○ _____
○ _____

25 SATURDAY

26 SUNDAY

27 MONDAY

28 TUESDAY

29 WEDNESDAY

- ○
- ○
- ○
- ○
- ○
- ○
- ○
- ○

30 THURSDAY

- ○
- ○
- ○
- ○
- ○
- ○
- ○
- ○

NOTES

01 FRIDAY

02 SATURDAY

03 SUNDAY

04 MONDAY

05 TUESDAY

06 WEDNESDAY

07 THURSDAY

08 FRIDAY

December
2023

09 SATURDAY

10 SUNDAY

11 MONDAY

12 TUESDAY

13 WEDNESDAY

14 THURSDAY

15 FRIDAY

16 SATURDAY

17 SUNDAY

18 MONDAY

19 TUESDAY

20 WEDNESDAY

December
2023

21 THURSDAY

22 FRIDAY

23 SATURDAY

24 SUNDAY

25 MONDAY

26 TUESDAY

27 WEDNESDAY

28 THURSDAY

December
2023

29 FRIDAY

○ _____
○ _____
○ _____
○ _____
○ _____
○ _____
○ _____

30 SATURDAY

○ _____
○ _____
○ _____
○ _____
○ _____
○ _____
○ _____
○ _____

31 SUNDAY

○ _____
○ _____
○ _____
○ _____
○ _____
○ _____
○ _____

NOTES

_____
_____
_____
_____